A Week on the Broads.

Four Victorian gents at sail in a Norfolk gaffer in 1889

Introduced by Michael Goffe

ADLARD COLES NAUTICAL

BLOOMSBURY
LONDON · OXFORD · NEW YORK · NEW DELHI · SYDNEY

Adlard Coles Nautical
An imprint of Bloomsbury Publishing Plc

50 Bedford Square
London
WC1B 3DP
UK

1385 Broadway
New York
NY 10018
USA

www.bloomsbury.com
www.adlardcoles.com

ADLARD COLES, ADLARD COLES NAUTICAL and the Buoy logo
are trademarks of Bloomsbury Publishing Plc

First published 2017

© Michael Goffe, 2017

British Library Cataloguing-in-Publication Data
A catalogue record for this book is available from the British Library.

Library of Congress Cataloguing-in-Publication data has been applied for.

ISBN: HB: 978-1-4729-4513-6
        ePDF: 978-1-4729-4516-7
        ePub: 978-1-4729-4514-3

2 4 6 8 10 9 7 5 3 1

Typeset in Bembo
Design by Nicola Liddiard, Nimbus Design
Printed in China by RRD Asia Printing Solutions Limited

Bloomsbury Publishing Plc makes every effort to ensure that the papers
used in the manufacture of our books are natural, recyclable products made
from wood grown in well-managed forests. Our manufacturing processes
conform to the environmental regulations of the country of origin.

To find out more about our authors and books visit www.bloomsbury.com.
Here you will find extracts, author interviews, details of forthcoming
events and the option to sign up for our newsletters.

Preface

My late father, Dr. E. G. L. Goffe of Kingston upon Thames, was the last
survivor of a group of friends who met at University College London. In
the late 1880s just before and after graduating and going their ways as
doctors, civil servants or just young men about town, they undertook a
week sailing a gaffer on the Norfolk Broads. Their adventures, documented
here, show them doing what young men like, and still like doing, living
life to the full, with sports and activities, the pub and plentiful contact
with the opposite sex.

As the last survivor of the group, the manuscript volume of this work
and its slightly earlier companion, *Camping on the Wye* were handed down
to my father and then on to me, and have been kept ever since as family
treasures. Various people, on being shown the two volumes, have suggested
that they were worthy of being more widely known, and in particular I
must mention and thank my sailing friend Tom Dehn and his wife Lorraine
who put me in touch with Bloomsbury Publishing, and Lisa Thomas of that
firm, who has guided me in the presentation of the books and overseen
their production.

The original volume is leather bound and handwritten in journal form,
interspaced with watercolour sketches on cartridge paper, of great skill and
humour, the work of S. K. Baker. He was also the author and artist of the
companion volume *Camping on the Wye* having been one of the group of
four to have taken part in the descent of the river Wye in a rowing skiff.
Baker had been I believe, a civil servant and a bachelor or certainly seemed
so when as an eleven-year-old, I was taken to see him by my father.

Of the other participants, I unfortunately know nothing, due to the fact
that my father was not among the crew on this occasion, though I have
photos of him from this era, sailing on the Broads with a group of lads
from an East End boys' club which was supported by University College
Students' Union, on a regular basis. In this edition we have tried to
maintain the appearance and characteristics of the original, but time as has
taken its toll and the watercolours have lost some of their freshness, but I
hope enough remains to give a true impression of this delightful work.

Michael Goffe

Introduction

The Norfolk Broads are a series of shallow lakes, interconnected by rivers and artificial waterways, occurring mainly in the county of Norfolk but just spreading into Suffolk. They were originally dug out by hand in the Middle Ages to recover peat, which was mainly used as a fuel, and was a very valuable commodity. A rise in sea level, which prevented the normal drainage through the rivers and into the sea, resulted in the diggings becoming flooded and created about 50 or so Broads, only some of which were navigable by trading boats taking farm produce and other commodities to the villages and settlements. Farmers, using small punt-like open boats called keels, were able to access their fields up the rivers and drainage channels, taking livestock, produce and materials such as reeds and rushes for thatching houses or corn stacks to and fro; larger versions carried a square sail, and ventured further afield.

The other typical Broads boat is the larger wherry, up to 50 feet long and capable of carrying about 30 tons of cargo. It has a mast stepped well forward in a tabernacle, which allowed the mast, which was counterweighted at its base, to be lowered. This carried a single gaff sail often without a boom at its foot. On approaching a bridge —and there are many of them on the navigable rivers — a skilled crew usually of only two was able to lower the sail and mast, carry the boat's momentum through the bridge and, on the other side hoist mast and sail all without losing way. They were used for taking goods and produce down to the ports of Lowestoft or Great Yarmouth, the two outlets of the broads to the sea, for onward carriage by sea-going vessels.

If there was no wind or they had run aground, the alternative method of propulsion was by means of a quant, a long pole with a round or square wooden board on the end to prevent it sticking in the mud, used to punt the boat. A skilled man could make a speed of two to three miles an hour, but it was hard work. Luckily there were a number of waterside pubs for slaking the thirst. Towing by man or horse was not practicable over any distance as the land, being marshy and interspersed with drainage channels, did not lend itself to the provision of tow paths as was the case with the Thames and many of the new canals created to serve the needs of industry in the late eighteenth and early nineteenth century.

The northern group of Broads connected by the river Bure and its tributaries is navigable as far as Coltishall and flows into the sea at Great Yarmouth. At one time an extension canal, the remains of which can still be seen, required several locks to permit boats to navigate up to Aylsham but not being profitable, fell into disrepair and was abandoned. The southern group of Broads is based on two rivers. The Yare and its tributaries was navigable from Great Yarmouth on the sea to Norwich, and is tidal on its lower reaches, particularly at Breydon Water, parts of which were dredged to keep a channel open. An artificial channel running southerly was dug to link the Yare to the southernmost Broad, Culton and the River Waveney which was navigable from Bungay to Lowestoft, the other outlet to the sea.

This then was the network of waterways, originally for working boats, that became a reasonably safe playground for people to enjoy boating, swimming, sailing, canoeing, watching the diverse wildlife and is the subject of this book dated 1889, concerning the adventures of five young men about town. Access from the cities was by the network of railway lines that criss-crossed the country, and it was said that no place in England was more than 20 miles from a railway station. This was before the onset of motor transport, and our group of friends, having taken a cab, horse-drawn of course, to Liverpool Street Station journeyed by train to Wroxham with a change at Norwich, where their chartered yacht, *Blanche,* awaited them with a professional skipper.

Up to about 1870, yachting was mainly the pastime of the more moneyed classes, their yachts ranging in size from 30–40 tons to large steam yachts that were professionally crewed and skippered with their owners and guests being taken about and occasionally being allowed to take the helm or pull on a rope. Some simply cruised, often to quite distant places, while others went from regatta to regatta, where if the crafts were suitable they would take part in the sailing races, the ladies often being left ashore or on the accompanying steam yacht. There were also sailing races for the local fishing and working boats in various places around the coast.

Beginning in about 1870 came the great Corinthian movement whereby amateur sailors got together and founded clubs in suitable places so that not only local people, but those who worked and lived in cities, could take part in the sport of sailing on the coast and inland where there were suitable stretches of water that could be reached by the rail network. Various clubs were founded incorporating the name 'Corinthian' in their title but also many others without. Where sailors get together it is inevitable that a competitive spirit will arise and racing will take place. At first this was informal match racing between two boats, then fleet racing which required a set of rules to govern the close quarter situations of fleet racing. One of the rules of the Corinthian Clubs was that a paid hand could be carried on board to help sail the yacht but he must not touch the helm during a race.

It was in this climate that sailing on the Broads became popular for the non-boat-owning amateur sailor or would-be sailor encouraged by ease of access by rail. The Broads provided a largely non-threatening environment, no rocks to cause a shipwreck and sinking and, if events got out of control, a usually muddy bank to ram with minimum damage to craft or crew. They also offered sailing that was quite taxing in order to navigate the winding channels, with the wind coming one minute from ahead requiring tacking to make progress and the next minute from astern with the prospect of a gybe to be feared in a fresh breeze and a heavy boom.

The first sailing boats for hire were converted wherries, where the hold was covered over and filled with sleeping bunks, a galley and tables, all made so that they could be removed at the end of the season and the wherry returned to her real role of cargo carrying. Being large and requiring experience in their handling, they were always let out with a professional skipper and sometimes an additional paid hand who would also act as cook.

Various boatyards started to produce a smaller and sportier type of sailing yacht and the typical Broads Yacht was developed. They had to be shoal draft, have a short stub keel with a maximum draft of 4ft so as to navigate the shoal waters, which meant a hull with limited headroom in the cabin. As a result the lifting cabin roof for use when moored up for the night was developed. *Blanche* the yacht featured in this book does not seem to have this arrangement as far as I can tell from the illustrations, as she seems to have adequate headroom without raising the roof. One illustration shows the skipper going forward through the mast bulkhead into his separate quarters in the fo'csle. The rig was gaff mainsail and a headsail set from a long bowsprit but no topsail. The mast pivoted just above the deck so that it could be lowered for passing under bridges. Her steering was by a tiller working a large spade rudder not attached to the keel, which meant she was a very manoeuvrable boat, answering quickly to the helm, very necessary in crowded constricted waters and a true delight to sail.

A few years ago four of us sailed a similar though modernised Broads Yacht. We set a topsail and had an engine instead of a quant for use if the wind failed. There was a quant that was used on the occasions that we ran aground or needed polling off the bank, which when not in use was tied upright to the stays supporting the mast. The four of us on board, all experienced and used to sailing on the sea, were greatly impressed at the handling of our yacht and how well it suited the Broads. We used this book as our guide and followed the progress of the Blanche, though we did not venture into the tidal waters of Great Yarmouth or Lowestoft, nor did we venture into so many pubs or have adventures with young damsels, as we had our wives on board with us!

I hope this book with its delightful illustrations will give great pleasure in the reading and perhaps encourage some to forswear the ever-present hire motor boats and take to the quiet progress of the sailing boat which allows one to see nature at its best.

Michael Goffe

The crew at Lowestoft Sep 4.

What might have been.

Saturday –
It was a fine afternoon on the last day in
August 1889, when two persons might have
been observed taking a chop each in one of
the palatial offices in Whitehall:

We will ask you gentle reader to see us off
at the G E Terminus.

What might have been.

EKB   G.E   G.E   C.E   W.E

The crew at Lowestoft Sep 4.

Saturday –

It was a fine afternoon on the last day in August. 1889, when two persons might have been observed taking a chop Each in one of the palatial Offices in Whitehall: —

We will
  ask you

gentle reader, to
see us off
at the G.E. Terminus

for are we not bound for that quiet
little village, yclept Wroxham in Norfolk
whence so many Broad loving tourists have
gone before.   A laughter loving maiden
and a gentleman of artistic tastes and
aforesaid maiden's companion were the
other passengers. We ran through a
tunnel, with all its mysteries, sketch on

left
is
before
and
the one

on right is going through the tunnel itself
Norwich is noted for its many beauties as
well as for
the Castle   and the Cathedral

After tea and sundry purchases in the company of Mr. E. who kindly saw us off, we took the train for Wroxham where the "Blanche" (our future home) was lying.

The Railway staff took down the cases containing our simple wants to the boat.

The master - Kett,   and Mrs. K saw us all snug for the night, and left injunctions to "wrap up well".

The "Blanche" at anchor

for are we not bound for that quiet little village
yclept Wroxham in Norfolk whence so many
Broad loving tourists have gone before. A laughter
loving maiden and a gentleman of artistic tastes
and aforesaid maiden's companion were the other
passengers. We ran through a tunnel, with all its
mysteries. Sketch on left is before and the one on
right is going through the tunnel itself.

Norwich is noted for its many beauties as
well as for the castle and the Cathedral

After tea and sundry purchases in the company of Mr. S who kindly saw us off, we took the train for Wroxham where the "Blanche" (our future home) was lying.

The Railway staff took down the cases containing our simple wants to the boat.

The master – Kett and Mrs K saw us all snug for the night, and left injunctions to "wrap up well".

The "Blanche" at anchor.

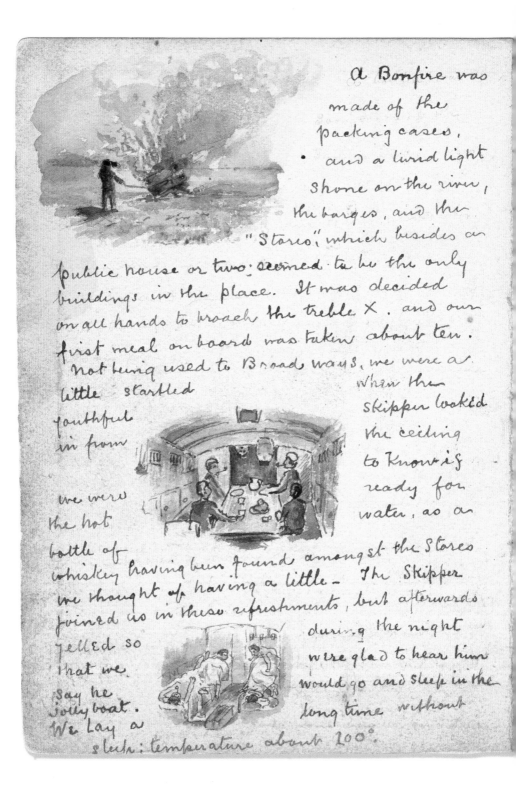

A Bonfire was made of the packing cases, and a lurid light shone on the river, the barges, and the "Stores" which besides a public house or two; seemed to be the only buildings in the place. It was decided on all hands to broach the treble X. and our first meal on board was taken about ten.

Not being used to Broad ways, we were a little startled when the skipper looked youthful in from the ceiling to know if we were ready for the hot water, as a bottle of whiskey having been found amongst the stores we thought of having a little — The Skipper joined us in these refreshments, but afterwards during the night yelled so that we were glad to hear him say he would go and sleep in the jolly boat. long time without We lay a

sleep: temperature about 200°.

The wind freshened, and the number
of knots became so great that we couldn't
wait to hear all that the fishermen
had to say; it was not complimentary.

Landing for a
Refresher.

A Bonfire was made of the packing cases and a lurid light shone on the river, the barges and the "Staves", which besides a public house or two seemed to be the only buildings in the place. It was decided on all hands to broach the treble X and our first meal on board was taken about ten.

Not being used to Broads ways, we were a little startled when the youthful skipper looked in from the ceiling to know if we were ready for the hot water, as a bottle of whiskey having been found amongst the stores we thought of having a little – The Skipper joined us in these refreshments, but afterwards yelled so during the night that we were glad to hear him say he would go and sleep in the jolly boat.

We lay a long time without sleep: temperature about 200°.

The wind freshened and the number of knots became so great that we couldn't wait to hear all that the fisherman had to say; it was not complimentary.

Landing for a Refresher

Always on the search for beauty (and beer)
G. + B. take the opportunity of a wait at a
Rail Bridge to get into jolly boat and
land at an Inn . They complained
on returning
that the
Barmaid
was suffering
from toothache,
and of the

quality of the Beer.

Dolce far
Niente!

Oulton Broad.

Always on the search for beauty (and beer)
G & B take the opportunity of a wait above
Rail Bridge to get into jolly boat and land at
an Inn. They complained on returning that
the Barmaid was suffering from toothache,
and of the quality of the Beer.

Dolce for niente!

Oulton Broad.

Preparations for Dinner.

Menu.

Poisson — Bloaters ; Legumes. Beans.
Turnips.
Potatoes
Pouding. Cornflour &
Jam.
Beer and Cheese.

Exploration.

Palpitation

" 'Tis sweet to hear the watchdog's honest bark "

Satisfaction —

Going for
Supper.
Farmhouse
near Yarmouth.

Preparations for Dinner

Menu.

Bloaters, Legumes: Beans, Turnips. Potatoes.

Pouding. Cornflour and Jam.

Beer and Cheese.

Exploration.

Palpitation.

"It is sweet to hear the watchdog's honest bark."

Satisfaction.

Going for supper. Farmhouse near Yarmouth.

We rose before dawn on Tuesday,
and reached Yarmouth at about 6, a.m.
where me landed for stores and a
Shave, besides a promenade on the
Beach, seeing in the Sporting Life also,
an account of the "presidents Jours". K.R.C.

W. and B. fall
in with a
Poetical
Skipper
who lures them
on board his
yacht, and then
and there assaults their
Ears with his lucubrations —

Effect of Poetry and Old Ale (one glass)

We rose before dawn on Tuesday and reached
Yarmouth at about 6a.m. where we landed for
stores and a shave, besides on promenade on the
Beach, seeing in the Sporting Life also, an
account of the "Presidents Fours." K.R.C.

W. and B. fall in with a Poetical Skipper who
lures them on board his yacht and then and there
assaults their ears with his lucubrations.

Effect of Poetry and Old Ale (one glass).

The Blanche had a race with another
boat and beat it, Then Horning village
came in sight and the children ran along
the shore scrambling for coppers and singing
some ditty about "John Barleycorn". We
anchored, or hove to, at a Ferry, where was
an Inn.

Horning
      Ferry.
    Here Kett left us and after a walk round we
started on our way to Irstead Shoals, the
journey was enlivened by C. blowing a horn
which seemed to rather excite a horse or two
on the bank as they followed us as far as possible

We were surprised to see a
large procession of youths in flannels
with umbrellas, making for an
enclosure with seats and a stand;
they turned out to be the "Lambs" —

We left these gentle creatures to the
Enjoyment of a double-barrelled
banjo performance, and after

The Blanche had a race with another boat and beat it. Then Horning Village came in sight and the children ran along the shore, scrambling for coppers and singing some ditty about "John Barleycorn". We anchored, or hove to, at a Ferry, where was the Inn.

Horning Ferry.

Here Kett left us and after a walk round we started on our way to Instead Shoals. The journey was enlivened by C. blowing a horn which seemed to rather excite a horse or two on the bank as they followed us as far as possible.

We were surprised to see a large procession of
youths in flannels with umbrellas making for an
enclosure with seats and a stand; they turned out
to be the "Lambs".

We left these gentle creatures to the enjoyment of
a double-barrelled banjo performance, and after

a stroll through the Market-place
got up the anchor and drifted
down to Breydon Water, laying
to at a small wharf

The evening was spent in strolling about, in bathing and getting vegetables at a cottage.

Itstead Shoals —

One of the party wished to get back to Norwich, so we rowed him in the dark to a village on Barton Broad.

His train having gone, he was lucky enough to fall in with someone driving there, who, the night being rather cold lent him a fur coat which might have been made for him.

a stroll through the Market-place got up
the anchor and drifted down to Breydon
Water, laying to at a small wharf.

The evening was spent in strolling about, in
bathing and getting vegetables at a cottage.

Irstead Shoals.

One of the party wished to get back to Norwich
so we rowed him in the dark to a village on
Barton Broad.

His train having gone, he was lucky enough to
fall in with someone driving there, who, the night
being rather cold lent him a fur coat which might
have been made for him.

Monday.

Towing
　the Blanche
　　　up to Irstead Shoals.

Lowering
　　the mast under Ludham　Bridge.

Preparing
　　　dinner.
onions potatoes
and turnips
tinned beef
and cornflour
　the fish caught were reserved for tea.

A narrow dyke leads up to the quiet and

picturesque
Womack
Broad.

Entrance to Womack Broad.
which was much
overgrown with
reeds etc

We got bread
at Womack Village.
where the
children treated
us to a selection
from "John Barleycorn"
this never fails to

draw coppers from the Broad tourist

Monday

Towing the Blanche up to Irstead Shoals.

Lowing the mast under Ludham Bridge.

Preparing dinner. Onions, potatoes and
turnips tinned beef and cornflour. The
fish caught were reserved for tea.

A narrow dyke leads us to the quiet and picturesque Womack Broad.

Entrance to Womack Broad, which was much overgrown with reeds etc.

We got bread at Womack Village where the children treated us to a selection from "John Barleycorn". This never fails to draw coppers from the Broad tourist.

We began to see some of the chief features, among the best of which are the Wherries, with only one sail they can go at a very fair pace, and are very steady.

St Bennetts abbey is a ruin with a windmill built in the middle of the spare stones.

These must have been brought originally from some distance, as the ground is mostly reclaimed marsh[a]. We stopped at Acle Bridge, about two miles from the village. The Broad Bridges are

a. Guide Book.

very flat like the country – Three little
Japanese students were on a boat here, their
skipper enjoyed a different menu, as he could
not manage to eat the same as they did, it
is probable that they could not join him
either when beer   was in the way.

" Three little Japs. from Town are we." –
They went on to Yarmouth, on WEd-nes-dee.

Mikado.

We began to see some of the chief features,
among the best of which are the Wherries,
with only one sail they can go at a very fair
pace, and are very steady.

St Bennetts Abbey is a ruin with a windmill
built in the middle of the spare stones.

These must have been brought originally from
some distance, as the ground is mostly reclaimed
marsh. We stopped at Acle Bridge, about two
miles from the village. The Broad Bridges are

very flat like the country. Three little Japanese
students were on a boat here, their skipper
employed a different menu as he could not
manage to eat the same as they did, it is
probably that they could not join him either
when beer was in the way.

"Three little Japs from Town are we."
They went on to Yarmouth, on Wed-nes-dee.

Mikado

Two of us went foraging for milk, and steering clear of dogs at a farmhouse we saw it drawn from the cow into our own jug.

Warm reception at Acle Farm House.

"Where have you been to, my pretty maid?"

"To get your un-skimmed King Sir,

She said

Nights dusky pall now fell over the heavens
and W and B. essayed to sleep on the floor
for a change. In the morning
B. was found squatting
thereon vainly endeavoring
to get that repose
thought by some
to be the labourers only
heritage, next day he tried a swim
in the Yare, and swallowed a mouthful
of ditch water, He never smiled again.
and was left in the
evening at
a hotel
in Acle
where the
Party spent
a pleasant
Evening
within a vine
grown Bar, Stories of the Broads, or
Broad Stories were retailed, The walk home
and songs, made another drink necessary.

Two of us went foraging for milk, and
steering clear of dogs at a farmhouse we saw
it drawn from the cow into our own jug.

Warm reception at Acle Farm House.

"Where have you been to my pretty maid?"
"To get your un-skimmed Kind Sir, she said."

Night's dusky pall now fell over the heavens
and W. and B. essayed to sleep on the floor for
a change. In the morning B. was found squatting
thereon vainly endeavoring to get that repose
thought by some to be the labourer's only
heritage. Next day he tried a swim in the Yare,
and swallowed a mouthful of bilge water. He
never smiled again and was left in the evening at
a hotel in Acle where the Party spent a pleasant
evening within a vine grown Bar. Stories of the
Broads, or Broad Stories were retailed. The walk
home and songs, made another drink necessary.

At this hotel a young lady was staying and took
breakfast with B. She was going round the Broads
with her

brothers
who
afterward
called
for
her.
It was
raining
at the
Bridge and
cooking was

rather a chokey affair.

Voice behind smoke.

How are you getting on, old f'la', Cook disgusted, Oh —

The rain clears and somebody
sings something about "Young
men taken in and done for"
the horn was brought out and
produced grand effect on bullocks
some miles away

At this hotel a young lady was staying and took
breakfast with B. She was going round the Broads
with her brothers who afterward called for her. It
was raining at the Bridge and cooking was rather
a chokey affair.

Voice, behind smoke. "How are you getting on,
old f'la", Cook disgusted, "Oh".

The rain clears and somebody sings something about "Young men taken in and done for". The horn was brought out and produced grand effect on bullocks some miles away.

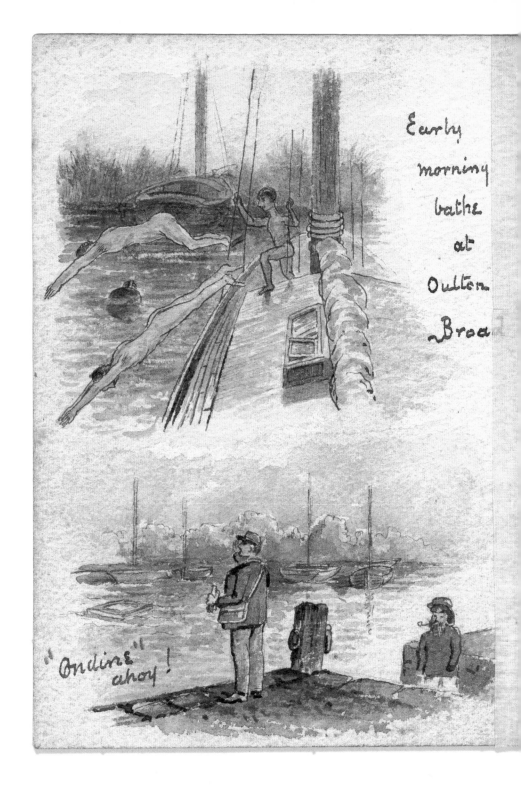

Early
morning
baths
at
Oulton
Broa

"Ondine"
ahoy!

Leaving Braden Water, after a long
chase we were caught at the entrance to
the Cut by a small yacht, sailed by one
man, we then continued on our way
to Oulton Broad, the tide serving
nearly all the way. The banks were
very high with tall reeds, and the
wind had fallen to a calm.

Early morning at Oulton Broad.

"Ondine ahoy."

Leaving Braden Water, after a long chase – we were caught at the entrance to the Cut by a small yacht, sailed by one man, we then continued on our way to Oulton Broad, the tide serving nearly all the way. The banks were very high with tall reeds and the wind had fallen to a calm.

Were just in time to see the above
transaction; and another bar of
"Young men taken in. etc was indulged
in by our crew, the tiller-man for
the time being then ran the "Blanche"
on a mud-bank (his thoughts being far
away) but after half-an-hour's "quanting",
the "putty" was left behind

The weather became
very fine, when the
party landed at
the Wherry Inn, Oulton
for a walk to Lowestoft
for the buying of
provisions, of
which we
were often
running
short.

The members were duly photographed (see page)
and some had a sea-bathe, the rest of the
time went very enjoyably, in lolling on
the sands, soothed to sleep by minstrels
and scared to death by menageries

Were just in time to see the above transaction;
and another bar of "Young man taken in", etc was
indulged in by our crew, the tiller-man for the
time being then ran the "Blanche" on a mud-bank
(his thoughts being far away but after half an
hour's "quanting" the "putty" was left behind.

The weather became very fine, when the party landed at the Wherry Inn, Oulton, for a walk to Lowestoft for the buying of provisions, of which we were often running short.

The members were duly photographed (see page 1) and some had a sea-bathe, the rest of the time went very enjoyably, in lolling on the sands, soothed to sleep by minstrels and scared to death by menageries.

Evening at the Wherry Inn. Oulton.

The liquids at the above tavern proving of the
right sort, we spent much time examining the
stuffed specimens, all local finds, as the worthy
host told us, including a goose from Egypt, &
a 40 lb jack (now alas very rare) W. with great
ability played some nocturnes on a piano, and
we were sorry when closing time came, and it was
necessary to get the Skipper out of the bar.—

Next morning our piscators wishing to catch a 40 pounder or two went forth in the dinghy and the rest went gaily car- eering up and down the Broad.

It was night when five persons might have been seen skirting the bye- paths for another walk to Lowestoft. "Good old beer", "To be there" etc, etc were sung in chorus, when the Moon came out to see what the row was about.

Evening at the Wherry Inn, Oulton.

The liquids at the above tavern proving of the
right sort, we spent much time examining the
stuffed specimens, all local finds, as the worthy
host told us, including a goose from Egypt, a 40lb
jack (now alas very rare). W. with quality ability
played some nocturnes on a piano, and we were
sorry when closing time came and it was
necessary to get the skipper out of the bar.

Next morning, our piscators wishing to catch a
40 pounder or two went forth in the dinghy and
the rest went gaily careering up and down the
Broad. It was night when five persons might have
been seen skirting the bye-paths for another walk
to Lowestoft. "Good old beer", "To be there" etc
etc wer sung in chorus, when the Moon came out
to see what the row was about.

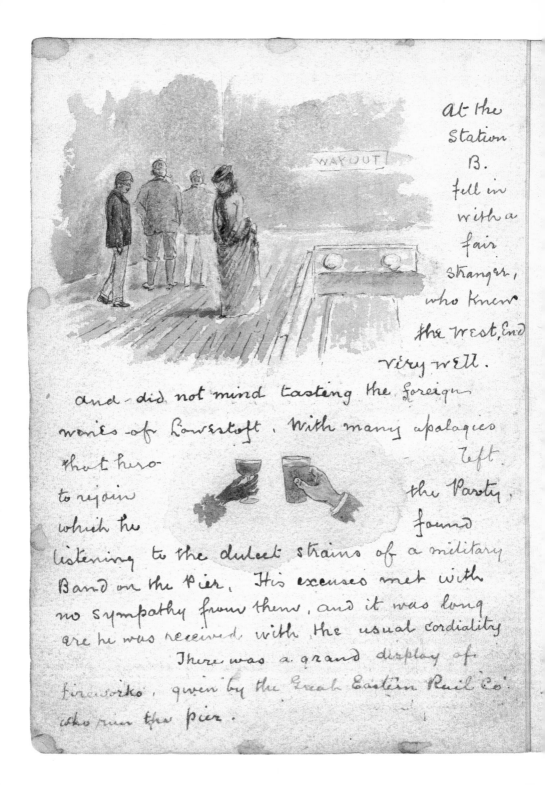

At the Station B. fell in with a fair Stranger, who knew the West End very well.

and did not mind tasting the foreign wines of Lowestoft. With many apologies that hero to rejoin which he listening to the dulcet strains of a military Band on the Pier. His excuses met with no sympathy from them, and it was long ere he was received with the usual cordiality

left. the Party, found

There was a grand display of fireworks, given by the Great Eastern Rail Co. who run the pier.

We spent the evening on the Pier with crowds of
people, watching the fireworks, and
admiring beauties of all kinds. The Band
stopped playing at ten, likewise the fireworks

At the Station B. fell in with a fair stranger, who
knew the West End very well and did not mind
tasting the foreign wares of Lowestoft. With
many apologies that hero left to rejoin the Party
which he found listening to the dulcet strains
of a military Band on the Pier. His excuses met
with no sympathy from them, and it was long
ere he was received the usual cordiality.

There was a grand display of fireworks given by
the Great Eastern Rail Co. who run the Pier.

We spent the evening on the Pier with crowds of people, watching the fireworks, and admiring beauties of all kinds. The Bands stopped playing at ten, likewise the fireworks.

Moonlight from Lowestoft Pier.

The night was very lovely and the whole
Party were sorry to leave; the last good byes
were whispered and the last train conveyed
us to the "Blanche" lying in her beauty on
the soft couch of the waters. We were glad
to be once more inside her woodden walls.

Be the roof never so lowly,

There's no place like Home.

Paying Toll
at
Railway Bridge.

Moonlight from Lowestoft Pier.

———————

The night was very lovely and the whole
Party were sorry to leave; the last goodbyes
were whispered and the last train conveyed
us to the "Blanche" lying in her beauty on
the soft couch of the waters. We were glad
to be once more inside her wooden walls.

Be the roof never so lowly,
There's no place like Home.

Paying Toll at Railway Bridge.

Frying
Onions.

Game of "Pitch Halfpenny."

Postwick Grove.   Some syrens on the bank called to us but
would not have a row in jolly boat which was sent ashore.
and pelted those who were in it with apples; wherefore
they returned unto the ship—

ruin
called
the Monkey House
near Norwick.

Frying Onions.

Game of "Pitch Halfpenny."

Postwick Grove. Some syrens on the bank
called to us but would not have a row in jolly
boat which was sent ashore, and pelted those
who came in it with apples, wherefore they
returned unto the ship.

A ruin called The Monkey House near Norwich.

Our skipper (Walters) distinguishes
himself by "quanting" in the rain.
We admire his skill — from
                    Inside.

A candle was stuck in the neck of a bottle, and we watched it
drifting away down the river Yare.

We turned into the cabin about 12. and had more songs
assisted by the skipper's " O for the golden wedding!" The
dulcimer came in very well for accompaniment and
being our last night on the Broads we kept up the
fun till early in the morning.

Our skipper (Walters) distinguishes himself
by "quanting" in the rain. We admire his skill
– from inside.

A candle was stuck in the neck of a bottle, and
we watched it drifting away down the river Yare.

We turned into the cabin about 12 and had
more songs assisted by the skipper's "O for the
golden wedding!" The disclaimer came in very
well for accompaniment and being our last night
on the Broads we kept up the fun till early in
the morning.

Emptying cask.
At the last anchorage.
Thorpe. Sep 7.

Bass relief
showing grief
of crew at
finding more beer
in the cask than they
expected.

Farewell to the "Blanche", and now up back-water
to Ketts' house, where tea and Mrs K. awaited us.

Miss Florrie on the look out for. W.

Emptying cask at the last anchorage. Thorpe. Sept 7.

Bass relief showing grief of crew at finding more
beer in the cask than they expected.

Farewell to the "Blanche", and now up back-water
to Ketts' house, where tea and Mrs K. awaited us.

Miss Florrie on the look out for W.

Row
round
Thorpe.
Sep 8.

We found the Ketts very hospitable, so much so that two of us decided
to stay over Sunday.

and W. became
somewhat
"gone" on
the charming
"Florrie"
who seemed
to be noless so

on him.

Their garden
was on the

other side of the backwater and we had several

visits over. going in a punt

This is what B. said he saw glaring through
a hole in the ceiling.

Sunday
Morning
at
Wroxham.

Mr Kett
arrived,
and we
bowled
down
Wroxham
Broad
in grand
style.

Row round Thorpe. Sep 8.

We found the Ketts very hospitable. So much
that two of us decided to stay over Sunday and
W. became somewhat "gone" on the charming
'Florrie' who seemed to be no less so on him.

Their garden was on the other side of the
backwater and we had several visits over,
going in a punt.

This is what B. said he saw glaring
through a hole in the ceiling.

Sunday morning at Wroxham.

Mrs Kett arrived and we bowled down
Wroxham Broad in grand style.

Trying a short cut
across Surlingham -
rowing not possible
water-way very
narrow and
several small
branches from
it leading nowhere

The
end of
Surlingham
Broad. and
no way out of it —

The Horn.
inspiring Hope.

Find ourselves near a Cottage and get help to carry
the boat, but it is too heavy and we follow directions
to a dyke leading to the River when —

The Blanche
at last. !
& Inn as usual.

The banks were very gay with bright flowers, the effect was very charming when a Kingfisher glided along in the shadows.

Florrie was kind enough to pin roses in our buttonholes on leaving—

The End.

Trying a short cut across Surlingham – rowing
not possible – water-way very narrow an
several small branches from it leading nowhere.

The end of Surlingham Broad and no way
out of it.

The Horn inspiring Hope.

Find ourselves near a cottage and get help to
carry the boat, bbut it is too heavy and we
follow directions to a dyke leading to the
River where The Blanche at last!

Inn as usual.

The banks were very gay with bright flowers,
the effect was very charming when a kingfisher
glided along in the shadows.

Florrie was kind enough to pin roses in our
buttonholes on leaving.

The End.